Satan
loves
TIRED
people

Satan loves TIRED people

BARBARA HICKS SEGUIN

Whitaker House

Scripture quotations marked (ASV) are from the *American Standard Version*, published by Thomas Nelson & Sons and International Council of Religious Education, and used by permission.

SATAN LOVES TIRED PEOPLE

Barbara Seguin
PO Box 3137
Center Line, MI 48015

ISBN: 0-88368-257-5
Printed in the United States of America
Copyright © 1987 by Barbara D. Hicks Seguin

Whitaker House
580 Pittsburgh Street
Springdale, PA 15144

CONTENTS

INTRODUCTION

This book is being written to warn people of one of the subtle devices Satan can use to slow down and hinder Christians — especially those who have made a firm decision to join God's army.

My experience seemed to begin suddenly, but I believe Satan put tiredness on me through a little crack that I had left open. Are you aware that demons need only a small space in which to drop thoughts into your mind? Tiredness can begin with just a thought: "You need to slow down" . . . "You're working too hard; you need to take some time off."

Satan also can cause you to think that volunteering for charity or church work is just too wearing on your physical resources. He can even give you the impression that someone is taking advantage of you, and that you are just too tired and burnt out to carry on any longer. He will drop into your mind some of the most unreasonable things you can imagine.

If you accept those thoughts as yours, however, then he can begin causing those things to happen. If you receive an inch, he will proceed to move in a mile!

Does this sound familiar? If so, beware. Satan may be mounting an attack on you. You may be having a psychological reaction to a mental image demonically placed in your mind. You need to make sure that thought does not become an action that will result in your being so tired you cannot continue to function in God's army.

Teacher and pastor John Wimber has said Christians' minds are "landing fields" for demons to parachute hindering thoughts onto.

On the other hand, you may need to have a complete physical examination. This is necessary to eliminate the possibility that your thyroid or blood sugar or other physical problems are not the cause of your suddenly feeling tired. It is preventive medicine and very important to have a physical at least once a year.

If you have not had one in the past year, let me suggest that you do so even before finishing this book. I want you to benefit from this teaching, but *I do not want Satan to be able to take the other extreme and convince you that you are not physically ill — if you are!*

In His name,

Barbara Hicks Seguin

1
GOD, I AM SO TIRED

"Oh, God, I am *so* tired! Why? Why? Why?"

I am sure that all of us have felt that way many times. We want so desperately to get off the merry-go-round of life and be able to just settle down a little bit.

We feel, "What's the use? Who cares anyway? Work, work, work, and never a 'thank you' from anyone. I am physically, mentally, and spiritually, tired, Lord. And if there is any other kind of tiredness, I'm that too. Please, God, HELP!"

Well, help is on the way for you. I hope reading this book will result in energy replacing that tiredness.

First, however, you must look for the *source* of your tiredness. Every thing has a *cause* and an *effect*. Tiredness is the effect of something that could be wrong in your mind, soul, or spirit.

9

A Mind Trap

Do you realize that your mind can be tricked into thinking the whole body is tired? This is a trick of the enemy designed to cause you to think your body is tired and burned out.

Singer Pearl Bailey was famous at one time for her song, *I'm So Tired*, and she actually found that she had to quit singing it because she became so bone weary and mentally tired.

You must think about the words you say. If you keep saying you are tired, then you will be tired. Pearl Bailey put that thought into her mind almost daily and soon tiredness became a reality. She wound up hospitalized. Only through counseling was she able to understand that her tiredness was a result of singing that song over and over, thereby "programming" her body to be tired.

She quit singing it and was totally healed as soon as she realized that through her mind's suggestion, her body had become ill.

If you are having problems along this line — and you know for sure there *is* no physical problem — then meditate daily on Isaiah 40:31. Your journey-ending tiredness will soon be gone, I promise you.

> But they that wait for Jehovah shall renew their strength; they shall mount up with wings as eagles; they shall run, and not be weary; they shall walk, and not faint.

Say this verse out loud daily so the enemy can hear it, and you *will* gain new strength and mount up with wings like an eagle and run and not get tired.

2
TIREDNESS IS A TRAP

Accurate communication is very important. To make sure that *tired* means the same thing to everyone reading this book, let's look at some definitions.

The *Random House Dictionary*[1] lists the definitions like this:

1) exhausted as by exertion, fatigued, or sleepy; 2) weary or bored.

These definitions suggest a condition in which a large part of one's energy and vitality has been consumed. A person who is tired has used up a considerable part of his bodily or mental resources. If exhausted, a person is completely drained of energy and vitality — usually because of arduous or long-sustained effort.

A person who is fatigued has consumed energy to the point that the body is *demanding* rest and sleep. A person who is wearied has been under protracted exertion or strain. Because the fatigued person has used up all of his energy, *he is burnt out*. Rest and sleep are the only solutions.

The exhausted, fatigued, and wearied person is in a trap and must break free. That trap is counter productive.

The apostle Paul wrote to the church at Philippi about one of his fellow workers who was in this condition.

> But I counted it necessary to send to you Epaphroditus, my brother and fellow-worker and fellow-soldier, and your messenger and minister to my need;
>
> Since he longed after you all, and was sore troubled, because ye had heard that he was sick:
>
> For indeed he was sick nigh unto death: but God had mercy on him; and not him only, but on me also, that I might not have sorrow upon sorrow.
>
> **Philippians 2:25-27**

We can see that Epaphroditus was most definitely so tired that he was burnt out to the point of death. Why? Because he overworked for Paul, his beloved brother in Christ, whom he loved.

But Epaphroditus put himself into that trap and almost did not get out of it. I do not believe God ever wants us to get to that point of tiredness. There must be a balance of spirit, soul, and body.

If this is the tiredness you have, God wants you to take rest and have peace and quiet. He wants you to be restored to your former self, to your former state of well-being.

Jeremiah 30:17 says, **For I will restore health unto thee, and I will heal thee of thy wounds . . . .**

Psalm 37:7 says, **Rest in Jehovah, and wait patiently for him.**

You can trust in the Lord. He is your source for the release of that tiredness.

In Mark 6:31, Jesus said to the disciples, . . . **Come ye yourselves apart into a desert place, and rest a while.** He knew that both he and his disciples needed rest. In verse 32, the apostle reports that Jesus and the disciples went away in a boat to a lonely place (a place alone).

The example Jesus gave us in this incident makes good advice today. If your tiredness does not stem from a medical problem, *take the advice of Jesus* and go to a "lonely place" to rest for a little while. It may be a good idea to take only your Bible with you and get to know the Lord a little better. This could be a good opportunity to build a better relationship with Him.

I would recommend a long weekend (at least three days and nights) at a cottage or a motel away from all the noises of the city.

If you cannot get away that long, take just three hours and spend them in bed. This is a good habit to get into every month, if possible. You will find your weariness and exhaustion beginning to leave.

Don't forget to take the phone off the hook. The telephone is one of the noisiest and most aggravating problems people can have in the world today. Yes, indeed, the phone can cause tiredness in you. Beware of that "monster"!

The Lord will restore your soul, if you will learn to lie down in green pastures once in a while. By *green pastures,* I mean achieving the tranquility of mind that would come through actually being in a green pasture.

> **Jehovah is my shepherd;**
> **I shall not want.**
>
> **He maketh me to lie down in green**
> **pastures;**
>
> **He leadeth me beside still**
> **waters.**
>
> **He restoreth my soul.**
>
> **Psalm 23:1-3a**

Visualize mentally the quietness and the peacefulness of being out all alone in a green pasture. This is what the Lord wants for you, if your tiredness is the result of burnout. The Lord wants to take that away from you, and give you new peace and strength.

Philippians 4:13 says, **I can do all things in him that strengtheneth me.**

Remember that you can do all things through Him Who strengthens you — if you are not burned out from the cares of the world.

---

[1] *Random House Dictionary*, Revised Edition (New York: Random House Inc.) Copyright © 1984.

3
BOREDOM CAN
BE TIREDNESS

Boredom is defined by the dictionary[2] as "the state or instance of being bored"; *boring* is defined as "to be weary by dullness, tediousness, or things done in repetition."

Many people are tired mentally from the dullness of daily routines. If there is tedious repetition such as seeing the same people and hearing the same conversations and doing the same things day after day, you can become tired.

This also is a trap. You become in bondage to the *boredom syndrome*. Boredom can sometimes lead to *apathy*, which is defined by the dictionary[3] as:

1) the absence of emotion; 2) lack of interest or concern; 3) insensibility to suffering; and 4) unfeeling coolness and indifference.

Now you could have some real trouble, if you do not snap out of the *apathy syndrome.* An apathetic person is easier for the devil to influence or control. Why? Because an apathetic person is indifferent, tired of everything and everybody. Usually, that person just kind of lays back and relaxes and lets life go on around him.

To get rid of apathy, you must get rid of the devil. The only way to get rid of the devil is to resist him, and you resist him by the use of God's Word. You need to begin to use the Word daily *out loud* so the devil can hear it.

James 4:7 says, **Be subject therefore unto God; but resist the devil, and he will flee from you.**

Therefore, all you have to do is totally submit to the Lord and resist that demon, and he will flee.

Otherwise, the *apathy* stage can develop into actual laziness — and that makes a person even more tired! This syndrome is like a cat chasing its tail: tiredness to boredom to apathy to laziness to tiredness. Beware if you are now in this trap. It is time to break out!

The Book of Proverbs has some interesting things to say about the various stages of tiredness.

> **He also that is slack in his work**
>
> **Is brother to him that is a destroyer.**
>
> > **Proverbs 18:9**
>
> **How long wilt thou sleep, O sluggard?**
>
> **When wilt thou arise out of thy sleep?**
>
> ***Yet* a little sleep, a little slumber,**
>
> **A little folding of the hands to sleep:**
>
> **So shall thy poverty come as a robber,**
>
> **And thy want as an armed man.**
>
> > **Proverbs 6:9-11**

God also admonishes us against laziness in Ephesians:

> **Redeeming the time, because the days are evil.**
>
> > **Ephesians 5:16**

The apostle Paul wrote to the Thessalonian church to not let anyone eat who would not work. (2 Thess. 3:10b to 12.)

Therefore, we can see from Scripture that tiredness which has moved into laziness will keep us from going forward in life. It will cause us to lose almost all of the impetus necessary to lead fruitful lives and to go forward in the race that the Lord wants us to run.

The idea I want to get across to you is that *energy makes more energy*. As you move about and set yourself in motion, this kind of satanic-inspired tiredness will begin to disappear as you gain momentum. As you develop new energy, it will increase and make more energy.

If you are tired — and again, if you are *certain* there is no physical cause — just tell the Lord about your situation and ask for help.

Just say, "God, I am tired, and I have gotten lazy, and I know it is from boredom," then *claim Philippians 4:13 as your promise*. Keep confessing that out loud again and again.

Paul wrote Timothy to *stir up the good things of the Holy Spirit that were in him* (2 Tim. 1:6a). The Lord has the same counsel for you. So go ahead and stir up the gift of God in you. *You* "stir it up" by using it, by making yourself go.

The best way to gain new strength is to pray in the Spirit daily. This edifies and charges us up. It renews our strength. We are praying for what we need and also for God's perfect will for our lives, but we must get our minds out of the way in order to pray rightly.

If you are into the syndrome of tiredness, your mind will send messages to your body that make you tired and lazy. But if you pray the Word and pray in the Spirit (to bypass your mind), then pretty soon, you will see results.

First, you must diagnose your case of tiredness or boredom; then, you must trust in the Holy Spirit to give you the remedy. He is our power here on Earth.

1 Corinthians 14:4 says praying in the Spirit *edifies* you, which means it "builds you up," and the same verse says that one

who speaks in an unknown tongue does not pray to himself but to God. You should make a commitment to pray in the Spirit *at least an hour every day* to build yourself up and give yourself strength to go on. If you cannot take that much time all at once, *take five minutes every hour.*

In Mark 11:24, the Bible says, . . .**All things whatsoever ye pray and ask for, believe that ye receive them, and ye shall have them.**

Therefore, we are going to believe that *you are going to walk in new energy.* As you move out and pray in the Spirit, you will obtain new energy. You will change those troublesome thought patterns. As you make your body move, you will develop a desire to keep on going and to grow.

Psalm 27:11 says, **Teach me thy way, O Jehovah; and lead me in a plain path.** Psalm 25:4 and 5 says:

> **Show me thy ways, O Jehovah;**
> **Teach me thy paths.**
> **Guide me in thy truth, and teach me;**
> **For thou art the God of my salvation;**
> **For thee do I wait all the day.**

Ephesians 6:18 says to pray at all times in the Spirit and to watch with perseverance and supplication for all the saints.

Yes, God said to pray for all the saints. A good way to get rid of tiredness is to make a prayer list and focus on your family and friends first, then on your country. As you pray for others, that tiredness will slowly pass off, because you are taking your eyes off your ownself and getting involved in other people's problems. You are "carrying one another's burdens."

Also, your age does not matter. Many people blame an attack of tiredness on their age . . . "Well, I'm not as young as I used to be." But the Bible promises God's people vitality in old age as well.

> **But my horn hast thou exalted like**
> ***the horn of* the wild ox;**
>
> **I am anointed with fresh oil.**

(The *horn* of the psalmist was a symbol of excessive strength and stately grace.)

> **They shall bring forth fruit in**
> **old age;**

They shall be full of sap

(which means "full of spiritual vitality")

and green

(which means "rich in trust, love and contentment").

Psalm 92:10,14

Therefore, no matter what your age, there is no reason not to have strength. There is no reason to let yourself believe that you have to keep this tiredness. God has the remedy.

You really are in a state of unrest, a state of aggravation over your condition, or you would not be reading this book. Your tiredness has caused an unrest in you. You are not happy with it. There is a remedy given by Christ in Matthew.

Come unto me, all ye that labor and are heavy laden, and I will give you rest.

Take my yoke upon you, and learn from me; for I am meek and lowly in heart: and ye shall find rest unto your souls.

For my yoke is easy, and my burden is light.

Matthew 11:28-30

Jesus is telling you that if you are tired because of a satanic attack of boredom or laziness, just to bring it all to Him. He can take care of that and give you the rest you need. *Tiredness is not spiritual rest.* He wants you to function normally and have His joy and peace, as well as to be a good steward and a functioning member of the Body in the area chosen for you to walk in for Him.

---

[2] *Random House Dictionary.*

[3] Ibid.

4

SPIRITUAL ENLIGHTENMENT

We have now come to the part of this subject where we must get enlightenment from the Lord. We must have a new *Source* Who will solve this lack of energy problem which is creating tiredness, which is creating apathy, which is creating laziness.

The Bible tells us in Psalm 18 that the Lord is our Light in the darkness.

> For thou wilt lighten my lamp:
>
> Jehovah, my God, will lighten my darkness.
>
> For by thee I run upon a troop;
>
> And by my God do I leap over a wall.
>
> Psalm 18:28,29

The Word is saying that if you believe in Him with all your heart, you can even leap over a wall. Do not doubt. Do not have unbelief. Believe that the source of your tiredness is Satan, but the Source of your enlightenment and your new energy is God. Accept this, and you can also "leap over a wall."

Jesus talked about a situation like this when the flesh is weak.

> **Watch and pray, that ye enter not into temptation: the spirit indeed is willing, but the flesh is weak.**
>
> **Matthew 26:41**

He knew that the flesh could be weak through tiredness, apathy, and laziness. Now that you know He understands, *you* have to make your spirit willing. The choice is up to you to make the spirit willing and to take control over the body and keep it under authority.

Paul wrote the Corinthians to **buffet thy body** (1 Cor. 9:27), and keep it under control. Do not let the body control the spirit. Let your spirit have full dominion over the body.

Just keep pressing forward. Every time your mind tells you you're tired, you tell it:

"Shut up, mind, in the name of Jesus. I choose to follow my spirit, and my spirit says I am not tired.

"Satan, you are a liar, and according to John 10:10, the thief comes to kill and destroy. But God has come to give us life more abundantly."

Just say that out loud every time the tired feeling comes over you, and the devil bothering you will flee. *That* is a Bible promise. It *will* flee!

Depression: Another Stage

Now, you may have progressed to another stage of tiredness, and that is *depression*.

Depression is a condition characterized by sadness, loneliness, and dejection. There could even be excessive depression, usually accompanied by feelings of worthlessness and self-rejection, as well as fatigue.

Sometimes, in this stage, people want to withdraw from reality. If this is your problem, I suggest you immediately talk to your pastor and receive Christian counseling. This area, or stage, of tiredness is curable just like the others.

However, if you are in a state of depression, then you need more help than we can give you in this little book. Pulling yourself out of depression is like pulling yourself up by your own bootstraps — you need outside help.

The purpose of this book is to illuminate your thinking so that you can modify your behavior in order to lead a more productive life. If you see that tiredness can be a trap, and that boredom, apathy, and laziness can be tiredness, then spiritual enlightenment will bring you into the area of change.

Once you receive this enlightenment, you can become a new creature in Christ. Once you realize where the tired feelings are coming from and that they are a tactic of the devil to slow you down or put you out of commission, you can stop receiving his attack. Satan works much easier with people who are tired and off balance.

God wants us to be filled with zeal as Jesus said in Revelation 3:19:

As many as I love, I reprove and chasten: be zealous therefore, and repent.

Another possible cause of tiredness is unconfessed sin in your life — from carrying around feelings of resentment to moral infractions. Tiredness will replace zealousness in that case. If there is any area in your life causing tiredness and a lack of zealousness for the work of the Lord, then He wants you to repent and get rid of it.

Read 1 John 1:9, and confess that verse aloud: **If we confess our sins, he is faithful and righteous to forgive us our sins, and to cleanse us from all unrighteousness.**

If the weight of guilt over some sin is keeping you tired, then repent and confess it, and He will forgive you. Then you will see that tiredness, apathy, or laziness depart immediately.

5
LEARN TO LIVE AGAIN

In order to learn to live with full zeal, you are going to have to clearly perceive what the devil has been trying to do. You are going to have to remember that he is attacking you mentally to hinder your Christian walk. You are going to have to be aware that he is trying to get a message into your mind that your body is tired.

Many times, a thought will surface in your mind, "You're too tired to go to the meeting tonight." But do not attempt to reason with the thought. Remember — if the little voice you hear in your mind does not say anything lovely or good or beautiful about the Lord Jesus Christ, then the devil is talking to you. Beware of Satan's tactics.

Another thing to remember is not to go by feelings. We are to go by the Word of God, not the feelings of the Body. Feelings can be another trap of Satan. Imagination can play tricks on you.

Have a Purpose in Life

Do you have a purpose for your life? Do you have short-range *and* long-range goals? Having goals is very important. If you have not set any, I recommend making a list of short-range objectives. Start with a week, then expand to a month and a year. Later, you can take future plans to five years.

You will find as you pray over these plans, using Mark 11:23 and 24, you *will* be able to say to that mountain, "Move!" And it will move.

Our first purpose as Christians must be to serve the Lord, to put Jesus first in our lives and family second. Everything else will fall into place properly, if we do that. Matthew 6:3 talks about renewing your mind, as does Romans 12:2.

> **And be not fashioned according to this world: but be ye transformed by the renewing of your mind, that ye may prove what is the good and acceptable and perfect will of God.**

To have a renewed mind means walking closer to Jesus. It means you have learned to be obedient. One of the main results of having zeal and more spiritual enlightenment in your life as you walk in obedience to the Lord's will is that you will have more peace of mind. Doubts will vanish, and you will not have qualms about getting through the day because of tiredness.

All of that will leave as you love God with all your heart and as you develop the mind of Christ and learn to think like Him. As you walk in love, you will find that satanic influences will not be around as often. The devil will never leave you alone completely, but you will be able to resist him.

You will be able to cross the Red Sea as Moses and the Israelites did. You will be able to live a more abundant life as you grow and trust the Lord.

Hebrews 11:1 says that **Now faith is assurance of things hoped for, a conviction of things not seen.**

You do not have to *see* what the Lord is going to do for you in the realm of zeal. You just have to believe and not doubt in your heart that He is there to give you new energy. It is up to you. You have the option to accept or reject the help of the Lord.

You have the choice of making a new life for yourself or staying the same. If you have had the tiredness syndrome, I trust that enlightenment from this book will enable you to have more peace and contentment and purpose in life.

God has a plan for you. You were made in His image. He is there to take you through the bitter waters of life. He is there to make those waters sweet. He is there to take tiredness away, and to do signs and wonders, miracles, and different kinds of works in your life — if you will let Him.

If you will completely turn your life over to Him, sickness and disease will leave. Because tiredness, apathy, and laziness actually are all forms of sickness. Through trusting in God and through the power of the Holy Spirit working in you, you can be a new creature in Christ, a new person.

You are going to be amazed at the new zeal you will have. Look at Psalm 30:2: **O Jehovah my God, I cried unto thee, and thou hast healed me.** Also in Exodus 23:25, the Word says: **And ye shall serve Jehovah your God, and he will bless thy bread, and thy water; and I will take sickness away from the midst of thee.**

Admit that tiredness is a sickness. Admit that it has to be bound, and then your healing will continue. As it continues, you will go forth with a new life. You will not be bound up. You will not be tired. You will look forward to each day, not in unhappiness as you have been, but with a new expectation of what is going to happen in your life.

Sometimes taking things for granted, being matter of fact about your life, leads to boredom. If you are bored, try walking around your home praising the Lord for everything you have.

I have done this. I have gotten to the point where I even thanked Him for my dishes, thanked Him for my bed, thanked him for every thing in my house from furniture to flowers. As you start thanking him, you will realize that everything you have is yours *because the Creator gave it to you.*

Yes, Satan loves tired people. But God knows that you are tired, and He knows tiredness is a trap and is ready to help. After defining tiredness and showing that it is a trap of Satan, we discussed the role of spiritual enlightenment. I pray you have realized Satan's trap and that darkness has gone out of your life.

Remember to put on the armor of God (Eph. 6:10-18) daily. Keep in the light of God by praying constantly and spending much time in the Word.

Then, to review this chapter: It is so important to have a reason for living. God needs all of us. *He is our reason for living.* As you thank Him daily and praise Him, try confessing Psalm 138:1-3 out loud daily.

> **I will give thee thanks with my whole heart:**
>
> **Before the gods will I sing praises unto thee.**

> I will worship toward thy holy
> temple,
>
> And give thanks unto thy name
> for thy lovingkindness and for
> thy truth:
>
> For thou hast magnified thy word
> above all thy name.
>
> In the day that I called thou
> answeredst me.
>
> Thou didst encourage me with
> strength in my soul.

Call on the Lord. He is always present and has a plan for your life. He wants you working for Him with all the zeal you can muster. He does not want His army incapacitated by tiredness.

Continue to believe Philippians 4:13 — **I can do all things in him that strengtheneth me.** Believe it, act on it, and in Jesus' name, I know you will be a new creature in Christ with new zeal and new purpose in life.

CONCLUSION

All that you need in order to say good-bye to tiredness, to apathy, and to laziness is the Word and the name of Jesus. No extraordinary faith is necessary to use the name of Jesus, just simple childlike faith in God and in the work of Christ.

So do not doubt in your heart but believe that those things you are asking for will come to pass, and you shall have whatever you say. (Mark 11:23,24.)

It is that easy: Say it, and believe it, and trust in His Word.

Certain psalms that we usually think of as claiming protection from threats outside of us also are promises for protection from things that attack the inner man. Learn these by heart, so that when Satan attacks with tiredness or any other anti-God thoughts, these promises will automatically roll out of your spirit in your defense.

The Word Is Your Defense

He that dwelleth in the secret place of the Most High

Shall abide in the shadow of
the Almighty.

I will say of Jehovah, He is my
refuge and my fortress;

My God, in whom I trust.

For he will deliver thee from the
snare of the fowler,

And from the deadly pestilence.

He will cover thee with his
pinions,

And under his wings shalt thou
take refuge:

His truth is a shield and a
buckler.

Thou shalt not be afraid for the
terror by night,

Nor for the arrow that flieth by
day;

For the pestilence that walketh in
darkness,

Nor for the destruction that
wasteth at noonday.

A thousand shall fall at thy side,

And ten thousand at thy right hand;

But it shall not come nigh thee.

Only with thine eyes shalt thou
behold,

And see the reward of the wicked.

For thou, O Jehovah, art my
refuge!

Thou hast made the Most High thy
habitation;

There shall no evil befall thee,

Neither shall any plague come nigh
thy tent.

For he will give his angels charge
over thee,

To keep thee in all thy ways.

They shall bear thee up in their
hands,

Lest thou dash thy foot against a
stone.

Because he hath set his love upon me,
therefore will I deliver him:

I will set him on high, because he
hath known my name.

He shall call upon me, and I will
answer him;

I will be with him in trouble:

I will deliver him, and honor him.

With long life will I satisfy him,

And show him my salvation.

Psalm 91:1-12, 14-16

It is so necessary to give thanks to
God daily. As you give thanks, he will

teach you to learn to live again. Psalm 92 is also a good one to read out loud daily. The Bible says that faith cometh by hearing.

The Word is living daily for you. All you have to do is open it up and declare it. Be diligent in your prayer life, and know the blessings that are yours. Deuteronomy 28:1-14 lists the promises that bring abundant blessings.